HELPING HANDS
Tidy Up Time!

PATRICE JOHNSON-MCLEAN

AuthorHouse™ UK
1663 Liberty Drive
Bloomington, IN 47403 USA
www.authorhouse.co.uk
UK TFN: 0800 0148641 (Toll Free inside the UK)
UK Local: 02036 956322 (+44 20 3695 6322 from outside the UK)

Because of the dynamic nature of the Internet, any web addresses or links contained in this book may have changed
since publication and may no longer be valid. The views expressed in this work are solely those of the author and do
not necessarily reflect the views of the publisher, and the publisher hereby disclaims any responsibility for them.

Any people depicted in stock imagery provided by Getty Images are models,
and such images are being used for illustrative purposes only.
Certain stock imagery © Getty Images.

This book is printed on acid-free paper.

ISBN: 978-1-6655-9813-2 (sc)
ISBN: 978-1-6655-9812-5 (e)

Print information available on the last page.

Published by AuthorHouse 04/22/2022

authorHOUSE®

DEDICATION

This book is dedicated to my lovely family, my husband Remeal Johnson-Mclean and my 5 children Caleb, Talia, Miriam, Joshua and Melchizedek.
"Train up a child in the way he should go, And when he is old he will not depart from it."
(Proverbs 22 vs 6)

ABOUT THE AUTHOR

Patrice Johnson-Mclean is a dedicated and fully qualified child educator. Pursuing a career in childcare since 2012, her desire to help children fall in love with learning by assisting with the growth of their developmental needs saw Patrice employed in a variety of entrusted positions – bespoke nannying, babysitting, crèches and roles in nurseries and primary schools – where she educated toddlers and children through age 12. Patrice is currently living in London, married with five children under 5 years old. With her childcare educator knowledge and practical experience as a mother she was able to use her first-hand experience to create the book Helping hands- Tidy up time which can be used by parents/careers to help encourage children to give a helping hand when tidying up.

ABOUT THE ILLUSTRATOR

Ramone Russell founder and CEO of LXR digital based in London was delighted to collaborate with Patrice Johnson-Mclean to create the vibrant illustrations for Helping Hands – Tidy up time. This is his first venture creating graphic designs for a children's book. We are looking forward to the impact the book will have on children helping to tidy up.

This book
belongs to

_____

 Trace your hand print above

Toys and colouring I love to play,

"Helping hands helping hands
time to use our helping hands"

But I have to remember to tidy away.

Shoes come in a pair, two feet left and right,

"Helping hands helping hands
time to use our helping hands"

When we come inside we must put them out of sight.

When clothes are not clean anymore,

"Helping hands helping hands
time to use our helping hands"

Don't just leave them on the floor.

When we sleep we rest our head,

"Helping hands helping hands
time to use our helping hands"

But when we wake up we must make our bed.

Top tips on how to encourage your child to help tidy up

- Extend the 'helping hands' catchphrase into a sing-a-long "helping hands, helping hands time to use our helping hands." This can be used as an indicator for your child to know it is time to tidy up.

- Use the book to have a discussion with your child on where they think the items on the messy page should go. Turn the page to reveal if they are correct.

- Give positive reinforcement – constantly praising your child as they tidy up will encourage them more.

- Lead by example - don't just watch your child tidy up but help them along as they do it.

- Give verbal instructions – don't just expect a child to know where to place items give them verbal direction on where things should go.

Printed in the United States
by Baker & Taylor Publisher Services